Praise for *Silvija*

"The stunning rawness and simultaneous devotion of *Silvija* is a rare find."
—*Canadian Literature*

"The poems in Sandra Ridley's book are potent and beguiling. Words are given the space they need to root and branch. This pace of them engages with the unarticulated, the hidden, the unbearable as readers encounter five elegies that allude to and invoke trauma, shame, and a profound sense of loss."
—Jury Citation, the 2017 Griffin Poetry Prize for Excellence

"Reading Sandra Ridley's *Silvija* is to be tossed into the beautiful, impossible web of language, so unafraid of darkness, so willing to bear witness, so brave in wrestling meaning from silence."
—*Pique Magazine*

"Ridley achieves a remarkable feat."
—*Winnipeg Free Press*

T0282036

Praise for *The Counting House*

"Constellating fragments from philosophy, feminism, and nursery rhymes, the book takes an unusual poetic accounting as it unfolds through wild linguistic leaps and startling juxtaposition. This is an ambitious and highly rewarding book."
—Jury Citation, the 2014 Archibald Lampman Poetry Award

"The diversity of language is marvellous, and Ridley's deeper humanistic concerns—about devalued subjects crashing forward into a condition of self-declaration—emerge through these poetic sequences intensely, and bravely."
—*Canadian Poetries*

"*The Counting House* is a powerhouse collection."
—*Cape Cod Poetry Review*

"In language that soothes and bites word by word, *The Counting House* is a book that lives fiercely in the complex in-between of love and punishment, pleasure and pain, coo and cry."
—Jenny Sampirisi, author of *Croak*

VIXEN

Sandra Ridley

Book*hug Press
Toronto 2023

Library and Archives Canada Cataloguing in Publication

Title: Vixen : poems / Sandra Ridley.
Names: Ridley, Sandra, 1973- author.
Identifiers: Canadiana (print) 20230223400 | Canadiana (ebook) 20230223419
    ISBN 9781771668569 (softcover)
    ISBN 9781771668576 (EPUB)
    ISBN 9781771668583 (PDF)
Subjects: LCGFT: Poetry.
Classification: LCC PS8635.I344 V59 2023 | DDC C811/.6—dc23

The production of this book was made possible through the generous assistance of the Canada Council for the Arts and the Ontario Arts Council. Book*hug Press also acknowledges the support of the Government of Canada through the Canada Book Fund and the Government of Ontario through the Ontario Book Publishing Tax Credit and the Ontario Book Fund.

Book*hug Press acknowledges that the land on which we operate is the traditional territory of many nations, including the Mississaugas of the Credit, the Anishnabeg, the Chippewa, the Haudenosaunee, and the Wendat peoples. We recognize the enduring presence of many diverse First Nations, Inuit, and Métis peoples and are grateful for the opportunity to meet and work on this territory.

For those who feel unsafe—

C ONTENTS

THICKET

You tried to talk some sense into her. You're going to get even, lying in wait. And soon it will all be over—your honey, your nectar, your honey flower. Hush, hush.

A little honey, wild clover, and nectar.
In a land flowing with clover and honey, you went to her nectar.
What is sweeter than honey. Worms after wild honey.
Blood and clover in her fur.

A curse.

✦

A land abundant.

What is sweeter than nectar in your mouth—
honey under your tongue.

✦

She fed you honey and blossoms and balm. And you came for her.

Caught—her honey remains but your scent does not.

✦

A fearful sight and a great sign—a streak of red
and it's frightening to fall by your hand.

You desire to make us few.

✦

In the bleak,
she fled from the ferocity and wrath upon her.

✦

As you take your fill, fill a wellspring with blood, as you fill the land,
the house fills with violence.

You take her fur, a curse,
an oath.

✦

And whosoever is of willing heart, you let them.
And whosoever gathers, you let them.

Whosoever receives the mark.
Whosoever comes after.

Whosoever denies.

✦

A cruel drink from the well.

And where there is no spring, no water, no river, she finds no rest.

Is there shelter?

There is never.

✦

And every one who would see her would shame her.
No grace in their eyes.

✦

And it sickens me, it does, and who wouldn't despair?
There are some who don't despair. I do not want to know them. I know them.

I do not want to know them.

✦

A scorch to the branches, a most vehement flame of buckthorn and fir,
a torching—as you stalk, eyes ablaze.

As if to terrify and it is somewhat terrifying.

Your fire will turn on you.

Before
the honey flowers
begin again
their blossoming.

✦

Clover and laurel and thistle
velvet and sumac
muskroot and sundew and baneberry
indigo and ironwood and primrose
crocus and cherrychoke
eyebright and bindweed
bedstraw and gentian and nightshade
moonseed and coltsfoot
panic grass and bloodroot and hyssop
loosestrife and boneset
goldenseal and sedge and lady fern
devil's bit and daisy and aster
violet and ivy—every leaf will wither.

You will suffer the same.

✦

The blossoms fall as dust.
And she, small as dust, for dust she is.
So say you.

The blossoms of the dust will cover you.
And your bones too will be dust.

Silver as dust, gold as dust—
ash falls
to the honey flower.

✦

After the trembling takes hold.

✦

A wicked plot to trap her paw—and your eye will have no pity.
Do you want dominion and to take pleasure?

✦

I feel no pleasure in the death of her.

✦

Wilderness—
a wasteland howling wild.

Unto the ends of the earth—
if an end will come for us, let it befall.

The end will come to pass.

The ends of knives, the ends of staves, the ends of traps.

Imagine that.

✦

She would tear off her paw to save herself.
This will not save her.

Imagine that.

✦

But what seek you?
Small wonder and amusement?

As you seek to lay hold.

As you seek her as she seeks to weep.
With each tree, with the forest, with the fallen.

✦

There is no end.

The stars withdraw their shining.

Your spark falls dark.

✦

And lest she be cast into a hole,
a deepening well, lest you want to slay her
in a hollow in a rock
or in a high place,
I become like her, cast into the hole.

Count all of us.

Creatures gathered, cast in the midst—
we fall as stones as our blood-spring
darkens with fear
and snow.

✦

Do not forget our cunning.

✦

Does she provoke?

Is she wicked?

In being wicked does she provoke, provoke to jealousy, provoke to rage?
Does even her grove provoke, provoke to wrath,
wherein each wicked thing
quickens anger?

Do you feel rage?

Blue and purple and scarlet.

✦

Torn to pieces.

Does she suffer? You ask not.

You come for the blood that covers you.

✦

And is it marvellous in our eyes?

Is it marvellous?

✦

Give sleep to our eyes, or slumber.
A little sleep, a little sleep or slumber, day or night.

We lie down with her to sleep a perpetual sleep on the fur of the fur.
Pangs and sorrows take hold of us.

Skin of the skin.

Flesh of the flesh.

✦

Quiet all the night.

✦

Who will escape?

✦

(She will sacrifice her paw to save herself.)

(This will not save her.)

✦

The waters will rise, and the sun, and in the midst of blue and purple and scarlet,
she will pull off her fur
and lift her head.

✦

After the trembling takes hold.

✦

We will tell everything—the words wild honey.

✦

All the creeks ran to the lake, to the valley, to the sea,
and all her rivers ran away as water,
and we to meet them—a blaze along the ground.
We ran to the well and drew blood
but would not exult it.

We ran to bear tidings, both run upon and after,
even as our eyes rained down.

And we said in our fury, let us run—we said unto ourselves,
let us not be weary for blood is a rivering.

And all the creatures ran from the fire and would not return.
And the creeks ran in our midst.

And our tears ran as judgment ran as water from the lake—
as tidings through the fire, through the fury, through the valley,
the river, the blood,
to the sea.

✦

TWITCHCRAFT

After your foxfire in our foxgrass—this ffoxerie, madness, woodness, wodnesse, wodnyss, wode. Find your woe. You fiend, you foe. Bewildered, you will lose your way, wandryng in our thykest wood. You must mask yourself to save your wretched life. After all, what is a lie? 'Tis but the truth in masquerade.

If he has a love for such, or if loathing did not prevent him.

A curse shall be in his mouth as sweet as honey as it was in our mouths, our mouths as sweet as honey. Revulsive as a flux of foxbane, as offal—and he will seem a lostling.

He came for blood and it will cover him.

✦

Each night my mother ran.

Each night the same.

The fields.
The long grasses.
Where could she go?

✦

A yowling.

And he seems a wreck, a wretch, a befouled bruise gone beyond indigo. He befits a spook, bleak before the old gunnysack.

Even as he is skinned alive, he raises his head.

Our howl becomes this brutal curse.

✦

They said he was the most violent man.
The most violent. And so I heard my father was the most violent man.

Each time different.
Never the last.

✦

Betwixt.

His body is a wicked shriek.

He withers, a nilling in a swithering of earthwood. He seems to sadden with cereuse. Averse to evers, he is transfixed.

But isn't the body a mouthful and a startlement?

✦

Nobody and no one and nothing.

What is normal?
What is home?

✦

The night gathers up into its body—if we can't inhabit, we shall haunt. In starlessness, his lanthorn lights a deadfall.

A lostling.

A thistle in the thicket, another russet masque in a skulke of ffoxes. He flaunts a sodden taunt, a blaze of tail. He becomes a ruddy thrall.

✦

Am I of [rape]?
I am of [   ].

From the have and the hold.

I sicken myself.

✦

25

It seems the unseemly and misshapen happens, hoodwinked by the night's kilter and tilt. He is caught in a lapse mistaken for a lack.

His dire bodykins anointed in dew, a keening panic, a lurk in the dark.

Askew in the eldritch, tufts of a fur tuft of what was a furred paw.

✦

You can't write that. Who cares if I don't.
But if I write about myself, will this draw you closer? By my self, I mean her, I mean you.

I mean us.

Plainly in a way that will not please.

✦

Unbidden, a spooklight, a nightmaker, he seems a nikin, a creature, a very soft creature—his underness, an unkanny prank of second sight.

Yet a fake and a fetch. Riven with affliction, with ravenous crookedness.

Hush, hush.

And sudden, a hocus, a harum-scarum, we mark him as swithen.

So musky and sleek.

✦

As if he would terrify, and he is somewhat terrifying.

Thou seeist?

Yes, you saw.

✦

And suddenly he seems a trifle, a phanatic, a phrantic, a nullity, a mere nothing, a phantom appearing a schismatic trick—

In foxsleep.

He seems a faltering, a mock, a folly under a dead eye.

✦

And he killed her, it seemed, he was so close to killing her, he killed her, and what about your brother, yes, him too.

We held our own.

✦

Come cur. Come torment. Come murmur. Come utterance.

✦

Come what may. Confess.

We run. We hide.

✦

Spark and cinder, he seems a fret, a fyre, moody fit for a scathing. And he keeps unkempt, a wretched scent. A starkened switch.

A stone in the mouth. Bristled maw. Unspeakable honey.

In the twitch of fern, we fur-line his whimper—he whispers a scritch.

✦

Come the end, he will stalk nothing.

And are we alive yet?
We are alive.

We will go forth with a wildering charm.

✦

THE SEASON OF THE HAUNT

What sweet vixen trick is this? A she-fox, a fixen, or, more anciently, a ffoxin— she plays the vixen with every wild thing about her. Just unearthed, see, here's her hole! She is a fool, a nasty queane, a slut, a fixin, a scolde, and oh, she is pestilent when she is angry and as proud as Lucifer, cross and snappish. A fire who raises her combustions to the world—

TALLYHO—*your vixen will run from daybreak to sunset*—we found our vixen and ran her upward of two hours, and after a circling run, she ran covert for a spell, her mask hidden in a dark patch of murkwood, then she crossed through the water and laid herself up on one of the rough tumps of earth and sedge, but when she took to her legs again, she was viewed, and after her two-hour run we killed her— we found our vixen, and we ran her at her full length, dodging, out on the surrounding hills, which abounded with coverts and dull clefts, and after she ran her ring, she pointed over the open for the copse, but her scent was far from good, and her course line broke, but we saw her run along the top of some wall for no more than twenty yards, where she resorted to her sly manoeuvre, and where and when the wall permitted her, she descended, as she was compelled, at a gateway, and she ran and reached the murkwood, rather distressed, and then our hounds killed her—we found our vixen, an old vixen of pale colour, and no doubt she had performed her same trick (though somewhat more successfully on previous occasions) as her haunt was the same spot, and when hunted she ran the same line of country, and by her device she escaped, but her device went undiscovered, yet still we killed her, and no doubt our vixen was dismayed for failing to escape—we found our vixen at [   ] Wood at half past ten, and forthwith, and at her best pace, she ran from us over to [   ], to [   ], to

[   ], to [   ] Wood, to [   ], then to [   ], where she was headed by our party coursing to [   ] Field, where our hounds slackened, until dragged and drawn, and about a mile on, they came from scent to her view, swiftly over to [   ], to [   ], to [   ], to [   ], to [   ], to [   ], to [   ], to [   ], to [   ], then to Little [   ], and on to [   ], and over to [   ], and to [   ], and under the cover side to [

], where our hounds came very close to her for near an hour, then far over to Cold [   ], to [   ], and to [

] Hill, where our hounds hunted her in her double hedgerow, where they found her in full view and ran straight for her, and after a chase of four hours and a quarter, over the course of which we ran through twenty-six parishes without going into any cover!, and from [

] to the furthest point, the run was twenty-seven miles, but the full circle tallied thirty-five to forty miles, and our hounds slept that night in the kennels at the [   ] Inn—we found our vixen in [   ] Wood, and after two hours of giving her the devil of our dusting, we ran her to ground in a small head of earths in that far-famed cover, [   ] Woods—*in the heat of pursuit, your vixen should be able to select such a sanctuary*—after a most brilliant burst of fifty minutes, we ran our vixen from [   ] Gorse up to the garden, where among some curs of low degree we found her and killed her—we found our vixen at [   ] Grass, and she was of a strong scent, and the hounds stayed close at her brush, before a burst over severe country, but she pointed first for [   ] Wood, then bent a bit left, over the driest part of the [   ] Enclosures and [   ] Fields, and at this point a hare jumped up in view of our whole pack of hounds, who were, at that time, cresting along with our vixen's breast-high scent, and they continued to run for a half-mile in the direction taken by our vixen, and the anxiety and the despair at this moment may be better imagined than described, as the pace of our hounds was so great that for us to get them, or attempt to stop them, would have been impossible, because, by god, sir, our hounds were also running hare!, and the unlucky hare, having found herself a little distressed, turned short across the field, while our gallant pack kept straight forward on the line of our vixen, and without one single hound deigning to look for one moment in which direction she ran herself off and out of the way, she ran excellent for forty-three minutes to [   ] Heath, then with four more minutes, the fate of the vixen… her death, proclaimed by our thrilling who-whoop!—we found our vixen, as it was reported that she frequented an open field and it may be remarked the weather was unusually wet, and in the vales, our vixen found no dry lodgings to resort to, so she took to the hills, and having selected a spot where she could lie secure from the midsummer floods, we discovered her in double quick time, and with our hounds soon at her, we ran her merrily over the road, by [   ] to [   ], through [   ] Bushes to [   ], to [   ] to [   ], and back to [   ] Bushes, and from there to Old [   ] Row, near [   ] Park, where, after we chased her for over two hours, we ran into and killed her, but she wasn't the only vixen we found that day in that turnip field!—

from the find to the kill, our vixen ran nearer to thirty than five and twenty miles and it was two good days' sport in one!—we met at [   ] but found our vixen near [

], and she ran immediately, and crossed [   ] Road close by the railway station, and passed [

], and kept the village on the right, as she made a strong point for [   ] Bushes, and her pace ran too good before she turned to the right over [   ], at the margin of [   ],

before she ran from us on the right, out of town, [   ] on the left, and over the vale and through the [   ] Bushes by [   ], and across the [   ] railroad, where we ran upon her in the open, a few fields over from [   ] on [   ] Heath, in a fine time of fifty-five minutes, but we found another, yes, sir!, a second vixen!, in the   [   ]   at [   ], and our vixen ran off fast through the park, and crossed the road leading from [   ] to

[   ], a half-mile on the [   ] side of [   ], and over the wall for [   ] Quarry, evidently intending to visit [   ], but being hard-pressed, she turned short before reaching [   ] Farm, and flew for [   ] Grove, and kept the [   ] on the left, over [   ] Hill, and across the [   ] Road again, to enter the vale to [   ], before she passed close by [   ], where she gained the wood by [   ]

Ash and ran straight to [   ] Down, having skirted [   ], which was a mile long with several earths, then she ran away parallel to make her valiant attempt to reach [   ] Wood, before she turned back for the village, before making her point of [   ] Gorse, though she pressed through and away over the [   ] Road near the turnpike, and after she left [   ] on the right, we pulled her down a wet field away from [   ], and this last run tallied for us one long hour and seventeen minutes, and the two runs united being two hours and twelve minutes, the whole at great pace, and it was for us a very severe day's work, and yet nothing short of the acme of our perfection would let us taste our second vixen on that arduous day—it's true, I may have once or twice in my life hunted a "put-down" vixen and once killed a vixen in an extraordinary manner—our vixen gave her burning scent, and after a sharp burst of about two miles, we killed her as she ran for a well-known head of earths—*if a vixen's scent is burning, the creature, when killed, will look like a hunted devil!*—we ran her fairly into a full cry—after her run exceeding twenty miles, we killed our vixen in the centre of a village, just as the good people returned from church—our vixen fell, pulled down in thirty-two minutes—we found our vixen fresh in the wood, and she ran away at tremendous pace, but still we quickly ran upon her, and held on to her, until our fugitive ran a long line, down by [   ], over

[   ] Hill, and nearly to [   ], but we killed her between [   ] and [   ], after a capital run of one hour and thirty-five minutes—we met a leash of vixen, and settled onto one of them, and ran her to ground in a low bank overhanging a quiet brook, and then we drew out the second, and in another hour's time, she too was brought to hand—we followed each vixen at a killing pace, and it was the wettest season, the bloodiest season, but it is always the pace that kills—

half the pleasure of the chase is giving the hunted creature her fair chance, of which a bagged vixen never has—but we cut her foot pad before we cut her loose!—on the night before, when our vixen ran in search of food, bonfires were lit along the hills to cut off her return at daybreak, lit by the human imps of the world below, like demons from the nature of their work, these coal miners paid little to light and tend the fires until our hunt was over, hundreds waiting on the hills! oh to hear their unearthly shouts and yells, mingled with the cry of the hounds when our vixen was viewed, as she found her way to her haven was blocked by the lingering embers of the fires—then we found our young vixen at five o'clock in the morning at [   ] Wood, on the edge of the largest woodland in the county, six miles from [   ], off the old [   ] Road, but we killed her close to [   ], a total of fifteen miles from point to point, but she ran a circuitous line, so her run was at least twenty miles, and our pace was tremendous, and none who started with the hounds still rode at the finish, and we ran with fifty couples of hounds—*feel how petrified she is, her heart banging away like hell*—yes, we possessed a bagged vixen who would run our hounds for half the season, until, with a little mobbing and manoeuvring, we would pick her up by her tail and save her before she could be endangered so we could reconduct her to her dungeon, to keep her for another day's torture, so our vixen would "do for twice," however after her last severe run, the hounds caught hold of her, but out of sight, Julyans grabbed her from their mouths, somewhat uninjured, and secretly cut off her tail and pitched her over the hedge, which, being also an awfully thick one, allowed our vixen to escape a very short distance, refreshed as she no doubt was by the galvanic application of Julyans' knife!, and after a half mile more of running, our hounds got once more upon her, and she was "killed" a second time, but when we pulled her out from the hounds, to cut off her tail, to present it to Julyans, who cunningly requested it…you can imagine our astonishment when we found that her tail was already gone!—we found our vixen and we killed her after a severe run of upward of an hour and a half, having run her woebegone to the ground— *yes! kill your vixen in the most handsome and satisfactory manner*—we killed our young vixen with spirit, but before she sank before us, she gave us her last shifts and artful dodges—we found our vixen deep in [   ] Wood,

and oh her terror, as she was made to fly, as the fires were lighted and kept lit all night, and so our vixen rendered shy and ran from her county and still we found her—as our vixen faced the north wind in her most determined manner, we killed her after fifty-five minutes of hard running, but we had a wretched ride of twenty-five miles to home—from the find to the kill, our vixen ran five and twenty miles—we found our vixen far away, and after taking her ring round the covert, she ran for [   ], at best pace, and without a moment's hesitation, she ran through the old covert, straight as possible to [
          ], and away to [   ], to [   ] Hill, and to [
          ], and nearly to [   ], but she veered right, where she gained the covert in which we soon found her, at [   ], but then she ran through it and again to [
          ], before she crossed the River [   ], where she failed to find refuge in [   ], so she re-crossed the river near [   ]

Bridge, and from there our vixen ran to [   ], nearly to [   ], where she turned to the right by [   ], with our hounds close at her tail, and again tried the earths at [   ], and, by god, sometimes when you get to your vixen, only red pieces of her remain— *sometimes your vixen is cornered and injured*—after the Gardens of [   ], and after a terrific run of four hours, we pulled her down near [   ] Woods, and this chase was upward of thirty miles!—a kit ran to ground and I saw him dug out to be carried into a nearby field where he was chucked into the air, and when he landed, the hounds tore him apart—we killed our vixen after a run of twelve miles in the mizzling damp and oh how we savoured vastly our amusement—*your vixen pursued will run from daybreak until sunset*—and yes, our vixen was affrighted, and hers was the most ravishing scent, and most burning, and it was the wettest season, the killing season—and again I saw that my vixen was no longer alive.

THE BEASTS OF SIMPLE CHACE

Bridle gate, rackway, gorse, rot, whin, coppice, scrub, crag, fen, furze, field, cleft, fold, peat, heath, hummock, thorn, crevice, holt, hole, rough, briar, grove, copse, hazel, furrow, hollow, bush, bed, hedge, hill, vale, bye-ride, barren, moor, dead cover—no good lies in them.

GRAY *The Gray is a common beast enough and therefore I need not tell of her making, for there be few beyond the sea who have not seen some of her.*

In the lapse of day or last light, take no heed of her, for she is not a beast who needs any great savvy to slay, for she turns quick to bay, or runs short.

She sleeps long when she sleeps.

Take leave of your haunt and hunt her down—

Till nigh she be overcome.

In the jacklight, the hollow, the thistle, the clover, the ochre, the fescue, the furrow, and the thicket—a blindfold. A little fur sewn into the seams? A touch of willow-bane firelight. Bare-shouldered. And still. Soft-mouthed. Of nothing, from nothing, to nothing. Stricken. How long have you been here? How long will you will to live?

Track and trace.

The greater and the less, the rawness of the senses, consciousness, and the Truths—cause and effect: one part threat and one part waiting. No way to resolve the terror.

He will never know their true names.

VIXEN

VIXEN *The Vixen is a common beast enough and therefore I need not tell of her making, for there be few beyond the sea who have not seen some of her.*

She is the most fiery beast and as malicious as the wylfen. And this is the truth: she gives a deadly bite. She is a nasty queen, cross and snappish—proud as Lucifer.

With great trouble we take her, especially when she is with whelps, for when she is with whelps, she keeps near her hole.

Hunt her with hounds—foxhounds and greyhounds. Catch her with purse nets or catch her with hayes, but know she will cut your weave with her teeth, as the wylfen does, but not as quickly. When she runs and sees she cannot last, she sinks to earth, the nearest burrow she can find, which she knows well. Dig her out and take her.

Trap her and beat her head without pity.

You know where you can find her.

Take leave of your haunt and hunt her down—

Till nigh she be overcome.

Soaked. Soaked. With what, you ask. With what. Sweat? Blood? A luminous darkness. No. Eyeshine. No. Eyebright. No. Foxfire. There is a blindfold and a loosening. A fur-lined brocade. A velvet russet. An effigy of fern, of lichen, and of bindweed. Each in its trembling particularities. A bindweed. A tangle. A thistle. A thornberry. A hollow.

Unruly, unseemly, unspeakable. Who runs? Who hides?

Who sounds the cry?

Beset. Watched. In fear. In fury. From the woods. From the holes. From the rivers. To the sea. If not for the chase, the quiet. If no quiet, the truth. If no truth, the trace. If no trace, the trap.

D
AMMULA *The Dammula is a common beast enough and therefore I need not tell of her making, for there be few beyond the sea who have not seen some of her.*

She will flee mightily and far from your hounds.

Where she can find no creeks, she draws to great swamps, or to meres, or to marshes. And she will come out by the same way she ran in—to ruse you again. She will want to seek shelter.

Ever undone.

Take leave of your haunt and hunt her down—

Till nigh she be overcome.

And you run, as far, as far from, as far as you can—with raw fear.

You gnawed through your own foreleg to free yourself. Run on three with the right dangling, through bone-land, through peripheral light, to save your life.

The trembling takes hold. What is difficult is spoken of as impossible. Some creatures. Many creatures.

All creatures are beautiful once they're gone.

HIND

HIND   ***The Hind** is a common beast enough and therefore I need not tell of her making, for there be few beyond the sea who have not seen some of her.*

She is a wonderfully perilous beast. With great pain shall a man recover if hurt by her, and so we say in our old saws: *after the boar the leech, and after the hind the bier.*

A hind abides in her heaths and her wastelands, more than her woods, to enjoy the last heat of the falling sun.

Take her with hounds—with greyhounds, with wolfhounds—take her with hind nets and with cords, with harness and with pits, and with shot—crossbow and longbow—and with gins and leather traps, and with strength, as I shall say again hereafter.

A hind is cunning to save her life.

Take leave of your haunt and hunt her down—

Till nigh she be overcome.

Fox fur sewn into the seams. There was a blindfold. So you slip into your darkening pines. Are your hands tied? Yes. And were you sleeping? No. You are awake, listening, and listening for footfalls. A snap of a branch. Are you running? No. You fell. Of course, you fell—your legs splayed into ferns. Was it day? It's night. It's day and it was night. There is a blindfold. And a snap trap.

Any part of any creature will be taken for the whole. Fur, paw, dewclaw, tongue, tooth, bone. Sweet qualities bleed from sweet features. The whole is taken for a part.

His threats are conditional. His conditions change. No condition can ever be met.

Come back home.

W ILKATT **The Wilkatt** *is a common beast enough and therefore I need not tell of her making, for there be few beyond the sea who have not seen some of her.*

She is many. And she is diverse. If the hounds peradventure find such a cat, she would not be long hunted for she soon puts up her defence or runs up a tree. And because she runs not long, I shall speak little of her, for in hunting her there is no need of mastery.

Her falseness and malice are well-known.

One thing I dare say—if any beast has the devil's spirit in her, without doubt it is the cat, both the wild and the tame.

Take leave of your haunt and hunt her down—

Till nigh she be overcome.

In whose woods are you sleeping? No. You are awake. In whose dreams? And in whose nights? As you turn your face toward the sound. The soundless. The unnamed. In whose woods do your footfalls rustle leaves?

Of course he said, *run.* And you ran. Do I remember when I think of it? How do you live? When you think of it, how do you live? Muslin and sere cloth, a ripped scarf. And there, a blindfold. In the havoc of aspen. Wolf willow, honey flowers, and a snap trap. Do you remember? The darkening. You are nobody and no one and nothing.

(And it sickens me, it does, and who wouldn't despair? There are those who don't despair. I do not want to know them. I know them.

I do not want to know them.) Who will double back and call her name?

ROE *The Roe is a common beast enough and therefore I need not tell of her making, for there be few beyond the sea who have not seen some of her.*

She is a little beast and goodly to hunt, for whoso can do it, for in truth, there be few who well devise her nature.

When she runs at the start, she runs with leaps and with rugged standing hair, and her tail crops up all white. But when she has run far, her hair lies sleek, not standing, nor rugged, and her tail will show not so white.

And when she can no longer run, she will yield herself to some brook, and when she has long beaten the brook, upward or downward, she will remain in the water, so that there is nothing out of the water but for her head.

Take leave of your haunt and hunt her down—

Till nigh she be overcome.

And so, a twitch and a lapse. Why are you sad? You could be pretty, my pretty, my honey flower. You could be pretty if you smiled.

Wrapped in scarlet, bound with scarlet, a threaded binding, fine and blue, but scarlet in its blue, her scar—he takes this and the birch and the hyssop, and spreads his cloth. She is clothed in scarlet, and her lips are threads of scarlet, arrayed and drawn. His fine linen, false indigo. Her scar, a shadow in the wellspring.

WYLFEN *The Wylfen is a common beast enough and therefore I need not tell of her making, for there be few beyond the sea who have not seen some of her.*

Take her with hounds—with wolfhounds and greyhounds—with nets, and with cords, but if she is taken with nets or with cords, she cuts them wonderfully fast with her teeth, unless you quickly slay her.

Take her with pits, and with needles, and with snares—with a haussepiez, jerk her from the ground by a noose—or take her with venomous powders given to her in flesh, or take her in any manner you can devise.

Take leave of your haunt and hunt her down—

Till nigh she be overcome.

Ravenous. Crookedness. This russet of dusk. Speak of this, in spite of this. There was a blindfold. In spite of this, what do you whisper when alone? Aubade. Again? Again. Close your eyes. Fern leaves, ivy leaves, leaves and leaves, the tilt of stars, and leaves, the living world.

Each season of dewclaw, fur, paw, thigh, tongue, bruise, and jaw.

Her blood-spring.

Snap through bone.

HARE
The Hare *is a common beast enough and therefore I need not tell of her making, for there be few beyond the sea who have not seen some of her.*

Undo all that she does in the night of her running. She takes flight for as long as she can, or she is already dead.

As she runs, she will not suffer any twig to touch her. Sometimes she crouches in the ferns, sometimes in the heath, sometimes in the corn and in the growing weeds, and sometimes in the woods. Hunt her in the morning and in the evening. It is a fair game to take her.

Slay her with snare pockets, with pit traps, with purse nets, with small nets, with pipes and long nets, and with small cords cast where they break small twigs.

Take leave of your haunt and hunt her down—

Till nigh she be overcome.

Afraid, you hid, hid yourself in the woods, fled and hid your tracks. In your hole, you hid yourself, and in the field, and in the brook, you hid in this lurking place. For a long moment, you hid for days and were not able to hide yourself when the woods were set afire.

Unruly. Unseemly. Unspeakable.

Thistle. Tangle. Thicket.

Thorn.

Look not in the eyes of any creature. The same creature runs with different names: wolf, vixen, vermin, heathen, honey, harlot, bitch.

G ILT *The Gilt is a common beast enough and therefore I need not to tell of her making, for there be few beyond the sea who have not seen some of her.*

Find her in pasture till all pastures fail her like hawthorns. She will run well and fly.

She slips out of the forest and when compelled she crosses the open country. When she runs, she makes few turns. When she does turn to bay, she will run upon us and menace and strongly groan. And for all the strokes or wounds that we can do to her, while she can defend herself, she defends herself without complaint.

She will spare for nothing.

Take leave of your haunt and hunt her down—

Till nigh she be overcome.

There was a blindfold. Seams of fur. The smallest eyelets letting in flickers of sere light. See? A circle of radiant creatures. Of nothing, from nothing, to nothing. No bindweed. The blindfold loose in the clutch of your hands.

If not the violence, the quiet. If no quiet, the truth. If no truth, the trace.

He knows where the body is.

TORCHLIGHT

There. Gently, friend, gently. Softly, here she slept. In this cover, cleft. Here she has been. There, there. Softly, friend, she has been here. Nigh, she was. So say sorry to subdue her, tame her. Find her. Haven. Hovel. Hole.

with escalating persistence   a life worth
living well a life worth continuing well a
life worth living well a life worth
continuing well a life worth living well a
life worth continuing well a life worth
living well a life worth continuing well a
life worth continuing well a life worth
continuing well a life worth living well a
life worth continuing well a life worth
living well a life worth continuing well a
life worth living well a life worth
continuing well a life worth living well a

Is
this violence
implicit or explicit?

&

Is
she
afraid?

life worth continuing well a life worth
living well a life worth continuing well a
life worth living well a life worth

&

continuing well a life worth living well a
life worth continuing well a life worth
living well a life worth continuing when
life worth continuing well a life worth
living well a life worth continuing when
even if you live the consequences outlive the
duration of harassment

doubted and   merely domestic in all
circumstances and in all circumstances
and in all circumstances and in all
circumstances and in all circumstances
and in all circumstances and in all
circumstances and in all circumstances
and in all circumstances and in all
circumstances and in all circumstances
and in all circumstances and in all
circumstances and in all circumstances
and in all circumstances and in all
circumstances and in all circumstances
and in all circumstances and in all
circumstances and in all circumstances
and in all circumstances and in all
circumstances and in all circumstances

Is
this harassment
"bad enough"
to allow us
to label her
fear
as reasonable and
this harassment
as criminal?

&

Does
she feel
a sense of dread
or a loss of control?

&

distraught   the pattern repeats

proper avoidance   and burden of proof
burden of proof burden of proof burden of
proof burden of proof burden of proof burden
of proof burden of proof burden of proof
burden of proof burden of proof burden
of proof burden of proof burden of proof
burden of proof burden of proof burden
of proof burden of proof burden of proof
burden of proof burden of proof burden
of proof burden of proof burden of proof

Does
she take steps to avoid
her stalker?

&

Does
she alter her life
to prevent the possibility
of his stalking?

&

burden of proof to establish your fear and its
reasonableness

actus reus his intention or tendency and his character and demeanour or your intention or tendency and your character and demeanour or his intention and tendency and his character or demeanour or our intention or tendency and your character or demeanour and his intention and tendency or your his character and

**Does
her stalker know
his conduct is unwanted?**

demeanour or your intention or tendency and your character and demeanour and his intention or tendency

&

and his character

**Does
she minimize
her risk?**

and demeanour or your intention or tendency and your character and demeanour or his intention or

&

tendency and his character and demeanour or your intention or tendency and your character and demeanour and his intention or tendency and his character and demeanour or your intention or tendency and your character and demeanour exposed

undeserving good and bad victims and good and bad victims and good and bad victims and good and bad victims and good and bad victims and good and bad victims and good and bad victims and good and bad victims and
Does
she tell her stalker
his conduct is harassing?

&

mens rea unrapeable

Does
she complain
promptly enough?

&

you are harassed

you want to walk alone you want to walk
alone you want to walk alone you want
to walk alone you want to walk alone you
want to walk alone you want to walk
alone you want to walk alone you want
to walk alone you want to walk alone you

Is
her fear
reasonable?

&

want to walk alone you want to walk
alone you want to walk alone you want
to walk alone you want to walk alone you
want to walk alone you want to walk
alone you want to walk alone you want
to walk alone you want to walk alone you
want to walk alone you want to walk
alone you want to walk alone you want
to walk alone you want to walk alone you
want to walk alone you want to walk
alone you want to walk alone you want
to walk alone you want to walk alone you
want to walk alone you want to walk
alone you want to walk alone you want
to walk alone you want to walk alone you
want to walk alone you want to walk
alone   day and night

S TRICKEN

Never-the-nere, this wide-where, this wild-mare, this mouth-maul. All-a-bits, all-and-some, all-to-nought, and high-alone—awayward to the back-o'-beyond. Your wood-mare, hearkening nearer.

Rejected Stalker ✦	Intimate Stalker ✦	Resentful Stalker
As in hunting behaviour courtship with intrusive contact and unhinged.	obsessional unwanted whispering	 and aberrant watching *she's paranoid*
Implied threats neuroses and delusions an anti-social personality a deep desire to frighten a trapped animal.	with or without with or without and and distress	following *he's following* a shell casing *she feels*
Or narcissistic and a lack of rage control with his need for revenge demanding	a catch song with callous effect and harm and insecurely attached a locket	with intense rumination carved her name into his arm a billet-doux a poppet.
Or persistent ironically fearful of abandonment antagonistic roughshod with fantasies especially violent	and jealous *he's going to kill her* and repugnant and aggressive	*he just shows up* *it's only a matter of time* before the violence appears.

✦

Predatory Stalker

He hid behind his horse to creep closer to his prey.

✦

Honey,

You don't see me.

But these days you hardly ever do.

✦

NOTES AND ACKNOWLEDGEMENTS

Out of the fire, bone. Out of the bone, light. Out of the light, longing—the hollow and the lack.

The epigraph for "Twitchcraft" carries three phrases adapted from other texts: *Wandryng in the thykest wood* is John Trevisa's (1387); *Thus must we mask to save our wretched lives* is Edmund Spenser's (1585); *And, after all, what is a lie? 'Tis but The truth in masquerade* is Lord Byron's (1823).

The epigraph for "The Season of the Haunt" also carries several phrases lifted and/or adapted from other texts: *What a Vixon trick is this?* is William Congreve's (1700); *Fixen… is the name of a she-fox otherwise and more anciently a foxin* is Richard Verstegen's (1605); *She plays the vixen with euery thing about her* is John Lyly's (1597); *The vixen's just now earthed, see here's the Hole* is Thomas D'Urfey's (1719); *She is a foole, a nasty queane, a slut, a fixin, a scolde* is Robert Burton's (1621); *She's a pestilent vixen when she's angry, and as proud as Lucifer* is Francis Quarles' (1644); *Vixons… who really do themselves embroil things, and raise miserable combustions in the world* is Isaac Burrow's (1687).

A pattern repeats.

Material on the medieval "hunt" was encountered in several sources, including *The Boke of Seynt Albans* by Prioress Juliana Berners/Julyans Barnes (1486), *The Gentlemans Academie* edited by Gervase Markham (1595), and *The Master of Game: The Oldest English Book on Hunting* by Edward of Norwich, Second Duke of York (1406). Details of specific aristocratic "chaces" were found chronicled in and adapted from *Notitia Venatica: A Treatise on Fox-Hunting* by Robert Vyner (1846) and *Records of the Chase, and Memoirs of Celebrated Sportsmen* by Cecil (1854).

An excerpt from an early version of "The Beasts of Simple Chace" appeared in *periodicities: a journal of poetry and poetics*, with thanks to rob mclennan.

This project was funded by the Canada Council for the Arts, the Ontario Arts Council, and the City of Ottawa Arts Funding Program. My appreciation to the juries involved.

Foxtails to wild ones and first readers: Amanda Earl, Phil Hall, Julie Joosten, Jennifer Londry, Lynn McClory, Christine McNair, Jennifer Pederson, Michèle Provost, Peter Richardson, Nancy Ridley, Su Rogers, Karen Schindler, Eric Slankis, Jennifer Still, and Adnan Tahirovic.

Coltsfoot and deep gratitude to Karen Solie, my editor, who carried a light through the murk of the dark. Asters to Stuart Ross, falcon-eyed copy editor; and daisies to Michel Vrana, book designer, who brought beauty to this work.

Vixen would not exist without Jay MillAr and Hazel Millar. For their constant confidence and support, bouquets of clover. I thank you and thank you.

This book is for my mother.

ABOUT THE AUTHOR

Sandra Ridley is the author of four books of poetry: *Fallout*, *Post-Apothecary*, *The Counting House*, and *Silvija*, a finalist for the 2017 Griffin Poetry Prize. She has won the bpNichol Chapbook Award, the Saskatchewan Book Award for Publishing, the Alfred G. Bailey Prize, and the Toronto International Festival of Authors' Battle of the Bards. Additionally, she has been a finalist for the Banff Centre Bliss Carman Poetry Award, the Ottawa Book Award, the Archibald Lampman Award, the ReLit Award for Poetry, and the Robert Kroetsch Award for Innovative Poetry. She has also been nominated for the Ontario Arts Council's KM Hunter Artist Award for Mid-Career Writer and for the Ottawa Arts Council's Mid-

John W. MacDonald

Career Artist Award. Ridley has taught poetry at Sage Hill Writing and Carleton University, and has had the honour of being a mentor with Ottawa's Supportive Housing and Mental Health Services "Footprints to Recovery" program for people living with mental illness. An audio performance of her chapbook *Lift* was presented on CBC's *Sound Exchange*. Her work has been anthologized and translated into German and French. Sandra grew up on a farm in Saskatchewan and lives in Ottawa.

COLOPHON

Manufactured as the first edition of
Vixen
in the fall of 2023 by Book★hug Press

Edited for the press by Karen Solie
Copy-edited by Stuart Ross
Proofread by Hazel Millar
Type + design by Michel Vrana

Fox woodcut image on pages 56-61 © 2023 by Cally Conway; callyconwayprints.com.
Used with permission.

Printed in Canada

bookhugpress.ca